The

BACKYARD

Book

VIKING
STUDIO
BOOKS

The
BACKYARD
Book

IDEAS and RESOURCES for OUTDOOR LIVING

Consulting Editor TRICIA FOLEY

Photographs by WILLIAM P. STEELE

Text by RACHEL CARLEY

Styled by MATTHIAS G.-F. MATTIELLO

VIKING
STUDIO
BOOKS

VIKING

Viking Penguin Inc., 40 West 23 Street,
New York, New York 10010, U.S.A.
Penguin Books Ltd, 27 Wrights Lane, London W8 5TZ
(Publishing & Editorial), and Harmondsworth, Middlesex,
England (Distribution & Warehouse)
Penguin Books Australia Ltd, Ringwood,
Victoria, Australia
Penguin Books Canada Limited, 2801 John Street,
Markham, Ontario, Canada L3R 1B4
Penguin Books (N.Z.) Ltd, 182-190 Wairau Road,
Auckland 10, New Zealand

First published in 1988 by Viking Penguin Inc.
Published simultaneously in Canada
3 5 7 9 10 8 6 4 2
Designed by Mike Rose
Produced by Smallwood and Stewart, 6 Alconbury Road,
London E5

Library of Congress Cataloging-in-Publication Data
The Backyard book.
1. Landscape gardening.   2. Landscape architecture.
I. Foley, Tricia. II. Carley, Rachel. III. Title:
Outdoor Living
SB473.B27   1988   712'.6   86-40600
ISBN 0-670-81666-3

*T*he young people may have rough and tumble play on the lawn, the father may feel free to don overalls and paint the garden chairs if the humour seize him, and the entire family . . . may frequently enjoy a meal out of doors with perfect freedom and naturalness. The plainest fare has zest when eaten *al fresco*.

    Neltje Blanchan, *The American Flower Garden*, 1909

CONTENTS

INTRODUCTION

Most of us have an image of our ideal backyard. Part nostalgia, part myth, it is a place composed of memories and daydreams colored by childhood fantasies, remote from the practicalities and cares of a real yard. Nevertheless, it is this image which we often unconsciously recall when planning and designing our actual yards and gardens.

Our enduring love affair with yards and gardens is a reflection of an instinctive desire for communion with nature. On the simplest scale, this is manifested in the colorful window boxes which appear on even the narrowest city ledge, but it can and has taken many forms.

As we traveled around the country scouting locations for this book, we discovered that many of the best, the most successful examples shared common goals. From a plucky little garden patio in a run-down inner-city neighborhood to an extravagant pool/spa carved into the side of a southern California canyon, these yards seemed at first to have little in common. A closer look, however, revealed that in fact their similarities were greater than their differences.

The uppermost consideration for many people is to use their space—whatever its size—to the fullest. A large family wants their small suburban lot to juggle a playground, basketball court, swimming pool, and storage for all the toys and sports equipment that they invariably accumulate. For a working couple's weekend retreat, privacy, tranquillity, and low maintenance are generally more important. A new house on a bland lot needs a fast injection of character. With others, the goal may be to capitalize on a beautiful view or hide an ugly one; to reduce noise pollution; to create a parking area for cars and bikes that isn't an eyesore; to shelter a pool or deck from prevailing winds.

In the pages that follow we have tried to capture some of the rich diversity and individualism in America's backyards. As these examples show, a successful yard is a versatile place that works gracefully as garden, outdoor room, and recreation area.

Yet while all these yards were designed to some degree to meet this goal, at the same time they express an essential artlessness—backyards are by nature unpretentious places. Generally, the formal flower bed has no place of honor here, and neither has the contrived symmetry of classical garden design.

If this taste for the informal has any theoretical origins, it is in the works of nineteenth-century American landscape architects, in particular the writings of Andrew Jackson Downing, architect of many famous gardens and parks. His legacy is still evident in the popularity of the naturalistic style of landscaping and in a preference for the asymmetrical and informal that are so visible in many of the backyards included in this book.

To the ideas of Downing, the work of the twentieth-century landscape architect Thomas Church may be added as a major force in shaping our yards. Church was a California landscape architect whose designs blended indoors and out in one space—the backyard. Here, driveways and patios, pools and decks were of primary importance; plants, shrubs, and trees served to link these separate areas and were only occasionally employed as ends in themselves. In a Church landscape, the focal point was the pool or the patio, not a manicured lawn edged with flower beds; the house and yard harmonized as a single living area; and the distinction between indoors and outdoors was broken down.

Most significantly, Church's designs employed a functional aesthetic that matched contemporary lifestyles. This practical, generally low-maintenance approach could be adapted to different needs and less clement weather than that of the California coast. Still, between Downing in the East and Church in the West, we can consider that the American backyard was born of both coasts and grew rapidly in popularity across the continent.

Today, most yards do not look for inspiration to any theorist: far more often they are sculpted to fill the dreams—and needs—of their owners. But while at heart the backyard conforms to few dictates of style or taste, general design principles still apply. Whatever the ultimate goal, a successful yard still employs scale, color, and harmony in much the same way as a beautiful garden or well-designed room. Here, however, the raw materials are footpaths, fences, driveways, decks, pools, and patios as well as plants.

Rather like the design of a room, the design of a yard very often has some very basic practical goals besides the obvious desire to enhance house and property. In fact, its design most often benefits from very specific goals, which organize and focus the planning that otherwise can lapse into a series of haphazard decisions.

In the end, though the ideal backyard we cherish somewhere in our dreams is immune from droughts, pests, and problems of all kinds, our own yards, thankfully, are neither as simple nor as boring as that.

THE EDITORS

S U B U R B A N

Y A R D S

*T*he elegant yet easygoing front porch is the backdrop for pleasurable meals and idle lounging. Bar Harbor-style antique wicker suits its romantic setting. In early spring, the native foundation plantings surround the porch with vibrant color.

THIS SPORTING LIFE

As pioneers of easy, healthy outdoor living, America's suburbanites were the first to develop yards into centers of family activites and interests. A classic example of that all-American prototype is this turn-of-the-century Colonial Revival set on an acre of sloping property. The house is geared to an active family with three children (plus half a dozen assorted pets) who spend much of their time together outdoors. As the family has grown, the yard has proven its versatility through the years, and now boasts an attached greenhouse, cedar deck, tennis court, children's play area, swimming pool, and vegetable garden, in addition to a two-car garage with the requisite basketball hoop.

Both architectural elements and landscaping on different levels bring character and shape to these diverse areas so that the property actually feels larger than it is. Plants also play a design role. Alongside the porch, hemlocks, rhododendrons, azaleas, and laurels screen the foundation, while taller evergreens along the property lines offer privacy from neighboring houses.

The generous wrap-around porch has been carefully restored to its original grandeur and furnished to period with antique wicker and a traditional porch swing; it acts as a comfortable, airy backdrop for informal meals and conversation in warmer months. And while the painted wood structure requires some upkeep—the southern side is prone to peeling in the sun—the owners consider it well worth the effort for the pleasure returned.

Close to the house, the play area for younger children is located within easy sight of the kitchen and porch. Here, regulation playground equipment was installed for both durability and safety. For graduates of the seesaw, there is a private playhouse atop the garage.

In the far backyard, tall trees shade the tennis court. The court has an all-weather surface, which needs only an occasional hosing down to rinse away fallen leaves. A separate water line was installed courtside to make clean-up easier, one of the many features added to make this hard-working yard as easy to maintain as it is to enjoy.

A true American classic, the porch swing hangs from early spring to first frost. Even after generations of use, it requires only periodic painting and a handful of pillows to be supremely comfortable.

*N*estled into one side of the backyard, the scalloped pool is large enough for family and guests. The flagstone surround is deep enough to accommodate impromptu clusters of furniture and water toys.

*T*wo generations of backyard play: the traditional climbing frame shelters a state-of-the-art tricycle.

With the simple addition of a basketball hoop, the asphalt drive becomes a family playing court.

*R*equiring little upkeep, the tennis court works well in a wooded setting, where leaves and tree sap can be a clean-up problem. The rust-proof, chain link fence has been rubberized in black to blend into the leafy background.

*A*n oversized thermometer, conveniently tacked to a tree trunk, gives swimmers and tennis players an updated weather report.

*T*he circular base of the driveway, visually relieved with a small pond and a few trees, will oblige the considerable number of cars, bikes, and toys typical of a growing family.

*A*t the back of the garage, a bluestone terrace raised on railroad ties offers an excellent vantage point for viewing family games— or a comfortable spot for a glass of lemonade.

PARADISE CONTAINED

*P*ared to bare essentials, this pure box of a cottage and its wonderfully plain yard demonstrate the wisdom of a seasoned gardener who knows where to stop. Recognizing that his tiny quarter-acre plot could easily get lost in masses of plants, the owner, Joel Dean, working closely with designer Jack Ceglic, shaped a design that draws its strength from profound simplicity.

The effect is immediately apparent. Precisely packaged by a hedge of tall junipers on one side and a trim privet on the other, the tiny house stands marooned with virtually no foundation plantings. But because the deliberate plainness emphasizes its importance as a piece of architecture, the cottage and its bit of front yard are able to turn a face of total self-assurance to the world, despite their relatively small size.

That same lesson in economy and balance extends to the backyard. To heighten the privacy, Dean and Ceglic chopped off the rear half of the drive and returned the space to the yard proper. The unused garage was rebuilt as a studio with a skylight and a washroom. Simply shingled to match the house, the little outbuilding blends in quietly on the back perimeter.

Equally understated is the back porch. Cleverly designed as a kind of oversized bench fitted with custom canvas pillows, it doubles as built-in seating and offers an appealing vantage point for the open lawn, which is kept bare of intrusions.

By limiting perennial beds to the property lines, Dean and Ceglic achieved a feeling of greater space than actually exists. To further enhance that illusion, the plants are graduated in height, starting with hostas, salvia, and silver mound, and then building up to taller lilies, seafoam, ferns, and hollyhocks as the yard slopes down. And while the overall effect is extremely reserved, the subdued palette of purple (ageratum, violets, sage, lilac, catmint, and leeks) and white (dogwood, hydrangea, wisteria, and daisies) provides just the right amount of interest against the cool green background.

A package of neatness, the 1924 summer cottage fronts the street on its unadorned lawn. A picket gate welcomes visitors with an enticing view of the back.

Fairly large when first planted, juniper trees lining the property edge grow about six inches each year.

Remodeled from a neglected garage, the studio takes advantage of previously wasted space. New windows offer a view of the backyard.

Tucked alongside the studio, the rustic grape arbor dates from the 1920s. Pruned for shape rather than optimum harvest, the vines are cut back on top and trained to trail over the sides.

The original driveway was cut in half to add privacy to the backyard. A picket gate allows a view while punctuating the drive's end.

Designed as a built-in bench, the back porch spares the yard from a clutter of furnishings. Canvas cushions can stay out all summer.

At summer's end the valuable Italian clay pots come inside, while their crop of purple catmint is transplanted to the garden.

A spreading rose bush is natural camouflage for utility meters.

*D*esign precision is evident in every detail of the property, as it is here in the copper bell against the copper front door.

ONE TRACT FIND

Suburban ranch houses have never won prizes for personality or inventive design: this 1960s model was once so bland that it was on the market for a full two years before the current owners signed the deed. But where others saw only a dull box on an ordinary two-acre plot, designer Joe Ruggiero and his wife, Barbara, spied potential.

In particular, they were drawn by the wonderfully secluded back area, surrounded by a sixteen-acre stand of undeveloped woods. Unfortunately, the house had been built with little regard for its pleasing site. But the Ruggieros were able to counteract this problem, typical of many tract houses, with sensitive landscaping and a simple deck design that opens up the entire back of the house to the cool, leafy yard. And, by taking care of the design and work themselves, the owners have achieved some big changes on a relatively small budget.

In the front, a new planting scheme layers colors and textures to soften the linear facade of the house, ease the transition up the sloping grade, and create a sense of anticipation near the entry off

*T*hrown over dowels, bed sheets make jaunty, informal canopies. The sheets can be easily changed for other colors and patterns.

*I*n one corner of the deck, a weathered lobster pot is now an ad-hoc side table.

the driveway. Carefully scaled, the greenery gradually changes in height from groundcover to azaleas and mid-sized shrubs to the taller dogwoods that screen the house without overpowering it, the way fuller shade trees might.

Even more effective in this makeover is the sixty-foot deck that runs across the rear of the house. With the connecting loggia-like sunroom, this generous open-air room is integrated architecturally with the house.

Deliberately and delightfully mismatched, the deck furnishings combine standard pieces with an unlikely cache of found objects, from lobster pots to driftwood. With his designer's eye, Joe Ruggiero

rescued these from the street, the beach, and even the local dump.

During summer, the deck is shaded with an ingenious canopy made from bed sheets draped over wood doweling. Around, accents of color are introduced through a "mobile garden" of potted plants that can be moved easily from deck to lawn as need be.

Although lush greenery and fragrant perennials belie it, the entire property requires only modest upkeep. A pair of juniper topiaries is the one indulgence of an owner who loves English gardens but has no time to tend one: purchased pre-shaped, the plants need trimming only twice a summer.

Accessible from the living room, loggia, and the bedroom, the deck is a relaxed and comfortable extension of the house.

*F*rench doors and oversized windows bring the outdoors into the brick-floored loggia behind the deck. Year-round afternoon sun makes this an ideal spot for potted plants during colder weather. The bamboo hat stand is an English antique.

A graveled area marks the transition between lawn and deck and is a shady spot for extra seating.

An outdoor shower, attached to the garage, serves the family from April to October. Rising steam from the shower brings out the scent of rose geraniums placed on the top of the stall.

Various potted plants serve as a portable garden, and, where appropriate, are wintered during colder weather in the shelter of the loggia.

ABIDING PLEASURES

As families grow up, the yards outside their houses respond to the changes from within. This well-trimmed yard has met the varied needs of the same family for over twenty years. It has, through time, accommodated childhood games, played host to a wedding ceremony, and welcomed a new generation of grandchildren.

Lately, the owners, who are now retired and able to spend more time outdoors, have added a well-tended vegetable garden and some specialty plantings such as young blueberry bushes for summer fruit. There are also touches that reflect special thought, such as the playhouse hidden inside an apple tree.

Besides addressing the comforts and interests of an extended family, however, the yard also responds in an unusual and interesting way to an extended neighborhood. The thirty-year-old house is located in a nineteenth-century residential park that was designed to incorporate private houses with a natural picturesque setting. This outlying residence is not part of the first park plan, but it does respect the original design of the community.

Because the town is so rural in character, there is little if any distinction required between public park and private yard. Here, set back from the street, the house is open to the road, while the yard spreads out without the hindrance of fence or wall. The full chestnuts, lofty firs, and knobby apple trees give the property an old-fashioned maturity that belies its relatively young age. The result is a well-used, well-loved yard that blends into a community that has been itself defined by a profound respect for nature.

A *canopy of wisteria shields the flagstone terrace from the nearby driveway. When exploding pods bombard their window panes with seeds come autumn, the owners know it's time to prune. Oriented toward the west, the terrace is used afternoons and evenings. Wrought-iron furniture needs little upkeep.*

The exclusive domain of visiting grandchildren, a playhouse is secreted inside a hollow apple tree.

A simple cage built of two-by-fours and wire netting protects young blueberry bushes from birds. Edging the vegetable garden, a similar fence keeps rabbits out. The slate path offers access while keeping feet off the plants and mulch.

WEST MEETS EAST

To visit landscape architect Ivy Reid at her snug California bungalow is to accompany her on one of her many explorations into the sunlit imagery of garden design. Specializing in theme gardens, Reid creates landscapes specifically suited to a particular house, its location, or the personal whim of the owner.

For her own tiny yard, about a quarter-acre, she has picked a romantic tangle of sweet roses, cosmos, honeysuckle, delphiniums, Queen Anne's lace, and strawflowers, secreted for complete privacy behind high hedges. The theme is a classic Nantucket cottage garden, to remind her of her home off the New England coast. And discovered unexpectedly clear across the country, the nostalgic yard is that much more delightful.

Like any cottage garden, this one finds its interest in color, variety, and texture rather than ordered formality. Freely mixed, the flowers are packed into enormous, wonderful masses, climbing in and out of a picket fence on the street side and bordering a rustic brick path in the back. And because almost any type of plant—shrub, vine, perennial, potted annual—has its place in a cottage garden, it makes an ideal testing ground for the designer, who can try things out in her own yard before recommending them to clients.

Finding immense pleasure in her garden, Reid has carefully oriented the house to take full advantage of this calm refuge. French doors open directly outdoors from the living room and kitchen, onto a shady brick terrace which provides a wonderful vantage point over the flower beds. All around the small property, thick fifteen-foot hedges seclude the garden, creating a sense of security while preserving the illusion of a New England garden come west. The difference, of course, is that here the pleasure lasts twelve months of the year.

Enveloped with honeysuckle, a tiny studio holds a library of well-thumbed gardening books.

Banking taller flowers behind ground-hugging impatiens and phlox strengthens the sense of enclosure.

*F*rench doors create an easy
flow between the living room and
the private terrace beyond.

*S*candinavian wood furnishings
on the private back terrace were
chosen for comfort and simplicity.
The petunia-bearing swan comes
from Nantucket.

A Victorian washbasin makes
the perfect pot for a pink
hydrangea.

*B*ehind a chair, delicate stems
of agapanthus, lively cosmos, and
fragrant roses form a living fence
around the patio.

*L*ate afternoon, at its most romantic, the garden is bathed in golden sunlight.

A SENSE OF COMMUNITY

One of the most influential ideas to emerge from nineteenth-century landscape design was the notion that the design of the house and surrounding property was inseparable. According to such influential contemporary tastemakers as the architect A. J. Downing, even the most modest residence deserved an attractive setting, no matter how tiny the actual property might be.

Built near the Atlantic seacoast in 1872, this Carpenter Gothic cottage and its yard epitomize this idea. The house itself is typical of Downing's cottage architecture: small and constructed of simple materials, it was specifically designed to be comfortable and attractive. The bay windows and two airy porches at the front and side are also architectural hallmarks of the era.

Equally characteristic of Downing's cottage style is the use of porches as the connecting element between house and landscape. Ornamented with whimsical jigsaw detailing, the shaded front porch looks across the property to the street. The side porch is more private and, with its view of the sea, is a favorite place for the owners to relax.

The rectangular corner lot is compact, but it has been designed to be an essential part of a composition that puts equal emphasis on house, yard, and the relationship of both to the street. As little as it is—about one-third acre—the yard is very much part of the streetscape. Heavy landscaping, which would tend to overwhelm the house, has been avoided. Plantings are kept low so that the eye moves uninterrupted to the tree-lined street. Reliable shade plants such as hostas and pachysandra flank the sidewalk in the dappled shade of the yard. In turn, a modest post-and-chain fence marks an understated border for the property.

*O*n a shady suburban street, the yard around this classic Gothic cottage looks much as it did when it was planned over a hundred years ago. The garage and functional gravel driveway, however, have been added, as has the hard-wearing concrete walk at the main entrance to the house.

*S*et into the back corner of its lot, the house presents two faces to the street and is approached by two footpaths. White azaleas and forsythia add sparkle to the simple garden each spring but otherwise much of the charm of the property derives from the lighthearted architecture of the house.

At one end of the property an old play house now makes a storage shed for garden equipment. By the front door a Carpenter Gothic box holds the day's mail. The original wood detailing on the porch railings is typical of this style.

A WELL-TEMPERED GARDEN

Suburban family yards must be many things to many people, providing outdoor spaces to meet diverse and evolving interests. Defining these different areas within a natural, low-key landscape was the primary aim for the owners of this sedate Georgian house and two-acre yard, set on a steep site sloping down to a river.

The result of a major two-year plan devised by landscape architect Randolph Marshall, the yard now takes advantage of its various levels to play up the dramatic river views while providing visual interest. It also works hard to serve a surprisingly varied range of uses—all within a wonderfully pastoral setting that resembles nothing so much as an English park.

Skillfully blending graceful design with more mundane functional features—garage, swimming pool, greenhouse, basketball court—the property satisfies the entertaining needs of two adults as well as the recreational imperatives of their four active children. With climbing roses, an abundant kitchen garden, and generous raised cutting beds that remind one of the owners of her native Great Britain, this yard also takes time to accommodate some personal pleasures.

The transformation, however, was not without thought and effort. The first major change came with the removal of several old fir trees and evergreens that were doing double damage by blocking out light in the front of the property and

obscuring river views in the back. Now, simple mountain laurels and blue spruce help soften and play down the more functional "public face" of the house in front, where a circular drive brings visitors directly up to the main entry.

The most dramatic landscaping was reserved for the private backyard, tiered in three levels for an elegant sweep from the house down to the river: uppermost, seating area and a grassy terrace opening off the house; at center, a classically designed swimming pool; and on the seating area and lowest level, riverbank gardens.

To soften the progression downhill to the river, the owners relandscaped with fieldstone retaining walls and small steps, and redesigned the existing pool with an unobtrusive bluestone terrace to help blend it more naturally into the hillside. By raising the ground level and installing tile drains, they were also able to completely transform the lowest level, which periodic flooding and constant dampness had previously rendered an unusable swamp.

This waterside spot now boasts lush perennial gardens, outstanding roses, a vegetable garden, and a few fruit trees. But it is the traditional raised flower beds that are a particular delight for their English owner. Her arrangements of fresh-cut flowers, displayed throughout the house, are a constant reminder of the pure pleasure this yard gives to her entire family.

The pristine white furniture surrounding the pool has a cool, clean look. For entertaining, extra chairs are pulled from their storage cubby in the retaining wall. The cubby is also fitted with an electrical outlet.

*B*reaking the yard into three
different levels has actually
heightened the romantic river views.

*G*olden, tranquil light at the end
of an afternoon slants across the
lawn (overleaf).

A BIGGER SPLASH

Skillfully grafted onto a steep tropical hill-side, this sleek landscape has all the exuberance of southern California at its flashiest: there are sizzling colors and cool contrasts, bright lights, cascades of water, exotic blossoms.

Yet for all its bravura, the design still manages to blend in convincingly with the surrounding canyon. Transformed by architect Luis Ortega from a nondescript 1949 ranch, the airy, pavilion-like house hunkers down quietly into a small valley. Above, a decadently lush growth of palms, ferns, bougainvillea, and lantana softens the hillside contours. Below, the multi-level pool with its underwater ledges and color gradation from pale blue to deep teal calls to mind the changing depths of a natural swimming hole.

Behind the pool, the tightly reasoned, geometric progression of stair and wall is a direct reference by Ortega to the work of Luis Barragan, the contemporary Mexican architect. The waterfall, too, is a Barragan touch, cascading over the cool green wall like a mountain stream to make a playful shower at the staircase landing.

Designed for entertaining, this sculptural pool garden is complete with a built-in barbecue, a raised fire pit, and an upper seating terrace fitted out with comfortable pillows and lounge chairs. With its intimate nooks and ledges and expansive circulation plan, the garden can make just a few guests feel at home or—in truer California style—just as easily accommodate many more.

Cool white stucco is juxtaposed against brilliant color in the small entry court.

Providing adequate shelter in the warm California climate, a new carport designed by architect Mark Enos fills in for the original garage, which was converted into a library.

Eight feet at its deepest, the pool evokes bottomless depths with underwater ledges and darkening colors.

The spare geometry and play of water against structure reflect the influence of Mexican minimalist Luis Barragan.

A wide sweep of staircase completes the circulation from pool and jacuzzi to the upper levels.

*T*he flickering flame of the fire pit invites guests to draw near on cool evenings. Both pool lights and waterfall are controlled by a master panel inside the house.

A sleek coat of plaster helps to incorporate the barbecue into the outside wall of the house.

RIGHT BY DESIGN

The guest cottage for an estate designed by the prominent nineteenth-century architect Stanford White, this dormered house and its expansive, park-like yard are now home to Long Island interior designer Carolyn Guttilla, her family, and her business. Although renovated to accommodate new elements—studio and connecting breezeway, a garage, several gardens, and two private terraces—the property reflects a sensitive effort by the Guttillas to adapt it for new use without sacrificing the spirit of the original design. Clearly, they have succeeded.

Secluded behind a dense growth of evergreens, the seamless lawns and an avenue of stately hemlocks lend the one-acre property the distant air of the private country estate—all the more remarkable given the yard's close proximity to a busy road. As in traditional old estate gardens, the classic design calls for controlled borders, beds, and potted flowers close by the house. Then, as the restraint breaks down and the landscape moves away from the residence, the lawn unfolds into a more informal scattering of firs, hemlocks, horse chestnuts, and fruit trees near the property perimeter. There, a bank of enormous evergreens forms a protective barrier, affording privacy from the road and muffling traffic noise.

To evoke further the mood of the old Stanford White estate, the Guttillas and landscape gardener Mary MacDonald made a particular effort to select plants that had just the right look and color—even scent—for the period. Garden beds bloom with a romantic mix of flowers whose names alone summon an earlier era: lavender, rose, delphinium, sweet alyssum. Similarly, clipped privet hedges, hydrangeas, and lush rhododendrons recall the familiar, wonderfully stodgy shrubbery associated with turn-of-the-century gardens.

Feeling the ultimate effect would be well worth the risk and expense, the owners succeeded in transplanting several magnificent hemlocks from within the yard, with a very good survival rate. And while the seventy-five-year-old boxwoods flanking the front door are an admitted extravagance, their old-fashioned fragrance proved irresistible.

Similarly, the terraces and new additions work to complement the original design rather than compete with it. In order to keep home and workplace apart, the studio was designed as a separate building, and a narrow breezeway smooths the transition between the two buildings. With its cupola and steeply pitched roof line, the new whitewashed garage is also virtually indistinguishable in feeling from the older estate buildings. Here the surprise comes in the interior: finished with recessed lighting, a sound system, and a *trompe l'oeil*-painted floor, the garage doubles as a party room. While standard garage doors close out the parking area, traditional French doors open on the other side to a private brick terrace beyond.

A stand of hemlocks makes its leafy, ceremonial way along the drive to the main house, while open lawns contribute to the feeling of an old country estate.

*O*ne of the many period plantings designed to fit in with the comfortable old house, this dense hedge makes an effective barrier between the entry garden and parking area.

*N*ear one column, a basket of lilies plays off the strict formality of a classical portico.

*F*itted with garage doors on one side and double French doors on the other, the flow-through garage doubles as an extra room for parties. Opening onto a secluded brick terrace, it offers wonderful views of the expansive yard beyond. The floor has been painted to look like the outer flagstone terrace.

*O*pening onto the flagstone terrace—one of two separate outdoor seating areas—a light-filled breezeway connects the house to the separate studio.

The terrace is a favorite spot for summer dinners, when the air is fragrant with an indulgent mix of roses, marguerites, and geraniums.

Late afternoon sunlight falls across a standard rose.

Automatically timed sprinklers prevent the lush lawns from becoming parched, and save the owners hours of tedious watering by hand each day. Instead, they often breakfast together outside, when the grass is cool and moist.

Rustic twig furniture from Maine is perfectly suited to the yard's old-fashioned country look.

GLITTERING PRIZE

When the working couple who own this sleek Mission-style ranch house set about renovating its typically bland suburban backyard, their aim was to create a center of outdoor entertainment to satisfy their own interests and pleasures. Anchored securely around pool, jacuzzi, and barbecue, that is exactly what their architect Brian Alfred Murphy's imaginative and indulgent one-third-acre design does.

Here, the undisputed star of the landscape is the fifty-seven-foot-long pool running virtually the full length of a raised tile terrace secluded behind the house. Although essentially functional in nature, the pool was conceived as an important aesthetic component of the overall design. It extends the length of the yard visually and does much to effect an air of calm and relaxation as it reflects dappled patterns of sunlight and shadow upward on the surrounding foliage.

Clearly dominant, the pool also acts as a refreshing focal point around which the rest of the space revolves. Just next to it, a jacuzzi is nestled into a tumble of rocks designed to blend more naturally into the surroundings.

A few steps away is an oversized, built-in gas barbecue, which has also been given a natural facing of cobbles and fieldstone. To more efficiently define the outdoor areas, the barbecue was moved from its original poolside site to a small flagstone dining terrace which now makes a more private spot for entertaining.

To unify the grounds around and beyond the pool, Murphy laid terracotta tile on the most frequently traveled paths; his wide steps at the end of the raised pool platform make a graceful transition down the graded site. Surrounding the yard, pretty border beds are thick with lantana, marguerites, tree ferns, and hawthorn, planted by landscape architect Richard Segal to help soften and extend the edges.

With the pool as their focus, the design team wanted to limit the fairly minimal gardens to the private border and a few small areas of interest within. The result—which belies the frequent care that keeps it that way—is a relaxed, easy look that reflects the owners' approach to outdoor living.

Moved away from the pool, the barbecue now has a more logical place by the dining terrace.

On a shady fence, oversized fixtures mark the time and temperature.

66

*W*ide steps double as seating at the pool's end. The shade trees are sycamores.

*S*mooth stones make a natural edge for the jacuzzi, tucked up next to the lap pool. Lilies, statice, marguerites, and gardenias create a soft palette.

*F*or an infrequently used path leading to pool equipment and storage, slate and moss lend color and texture to the walk (overleaf).

67

CITY

YARDS

TOUCHSTONE TO NATURE

The essence of any garden, small or large, derives from our basic need for contact with nature. For one couple, moving from the rural setting of a New England farmhouse, this desire was so strong that they went to work renovating their run-down city yard long before taking hammer and nail to the house itself.

Inspired by the success of two neighboring families—whose thriving front yards do much to brighten the city block—they turned first to the small garden fronting their Victorian row house. Now masses of irises, alliums, peonies, and roses bloom in brilliant purples, reds, and blues to enliven the entrance.

Next came the private yard behind the house, where the owners chose to follow a more formal design in order to organize most effectively the limited space. Influenced by gardens they had admired on trips to Europe, they based the new plan on a parterre, a traditional landscape technique that employs hedges, paving, pools, lawns, and other elements to divide and order an area in a geometric pattern.

The main framework for their parterre is an intersecting series of brick and gravel paths that define several separate rectangular beds planted with flowers and vegetables. In each bed something wonderful grows: there are peonies and miniature roses, foxgloves and poppies, herbs such as lavender and parsley, raspberries, and a peach tree.

Space is used to the fullest in this compact scheme: against a trellis a pear tree is espaliered, following the centuries-old garden principle that fruit will ripen more quickly in the warmth and shelter of a sunny wall. Nearby, a small sunken lily pond was constructed from two old bathtubs found in the house.

Typically, a parterre is most effective when seen from above. There are refreshing views of the yard not only from the upstairs windows of the house but also from a deck built off the kitchen, one story above ground level. With this addition the owners gained a comfortable place for eating and entertaining during warm weather.

Not all the views, however, are lovely ones. Facing the yard at the rear is a tenement wall, and the next project will probably be to increase privacy, an inescapable need in a city garden.

*S*unk into the ground, two bathtubs salvaged from the house make an ornamental pond where goldfish earn their keep by eating insects. A large slab of slate, found in the yard, acts as a bridge between the two ponds.

*T*he rear windows and raised deck offer some of the best views of the parterre arrangement. To increase the illusion of space, the owners used materials compatible with the yards on either side of theirs. For the deck they chose no-care fiberglass furniture that can be left outdoors in winter to minimize storage problems.

Shared by neighbors, a two-sided toolshed is fitted with pegboard for easy, inexpensive storage.

The parterre plan creates plenty of areas of interest for such a small yard. In one corner, young peaches ripen on the tree; color is introduced by the tall spikes of foxgloves and the purple flowers of chives; a cast-iron sculpture and the ponds provide accents to the scheme; and even in the shade of the overhanging deck evergreens thrive.

A Play in Three Acts

Wedged improbably into a crowded hillside in a Los Angeles suburb, this airy, light-filled house and its secluded yard are a welcome interlude of privacy and space amid the area's urban sprawl. Moreover, they manage to preserve all of the city's wonderful quirkiness and none of its chaos, a happy residual of the careful design of architect Fred Fisher and landscape architect Charles Pearson.

With its unlikely amalgam of materials and styles—sort of a cross between a Spanish hacienda and a Cape Cod cottage—the multi-level house is appealingly eccentric. As if to mimic the house's changing personality, the yard too goes its own idiosyncratic way, shaping three distinctly different, separate areas that are delightfully suited to the owners, a couple with young children.

The first is the very ordered front yard, a kind of grassy entrance court comprising a trim path, manicured lawn, and a sunny brick terrace. All rests calmly, enclosed behind a whitewashed wall that shelters the focus of the front area: a year-round vegetable garden irrigated by an ingenious system of cistern and valves.

By contrast, the sandstone side yard, bounded by a cool, sleek expanse of plastered wall, is completely bare of plants. Shady and very private, the space was conceived by Pearson as a quiet spot for contemplation. But it also doubles as an entertaining area: inventive built-in wall ledges are just the right height to serve as extra seating.

Finally, there is the more relaxed, casually planted back area, tucked amid a shady grove of eucalyptus trees. This quiet spot accommodates the children's sandbox, a dining terrace, and a naturalistic, pond-like jacuzzi, all integrated by a series of fieldstone terraces and retaining walls. So, while the yard is specifically geared toward active family interests, its overall look, amid lush ferns, towering trees, and natural quarry stone, resembles nothing so much as a bit of California woods transplanted.

A natural extension of the front stoop, the brick terrace becomes an afternoon sunning spot. Above, a rooftop deck yields views of the nearby Pacific.

Behind high walls, a secluded California yard comes as a calm surprise against the urban backdrop.

*B*ased on systems once used in California citrus groves, the garden aqueduct combines a copper cistern with a concrete trough, where adjustable valves direct the water flow to various furrows.

*A*n espalier of mature pear trees creates a rich tapestry of green to soften the garage wall.

*S*pilling from a concrete trough, a natural waterfall keeps the jacuzzi full. Cool blue tiles mask a prefabricated fiberglass form. The stacked quarry stone wall provides natural seating for shower rinse-offs.

*B*ougainvillea, agapanthus, plumbago, and sweet gardenias make a lush backdrop for the dining area, defined by a brick retaining wall.

In the quiet side yard, a quarry stone band traces a symbolic "stream" from the cistern in the front yard to the pool-like jacuzzi in the rear.

Backed by a stacked stone retaining wall, the semi-circular sandbox blends naturally into the yard. Dark green paint camouflages the cinderblock wall behind.

The careful design of perennials frames the backyard with a delicate yet rich palette. Toward the patio, the simply-constructed pond—a small hole lined with plastic sheeting—needs little upkeep: it is naturally filtered by aquatic plants and a few resident goldfish.

Dramatic foxglove, a self-sowing perennial, blooms in soft color.

GRACE UNDER PRESSURE

Perhaps nowhere is a garden more welcome than in a city, where even the smallest patch of greenery can be an effective sanctuary from the demands of urban life. That goal was foremost when the owners bought this house five years ago, for they found a property that had suffered from years of decay and neglect. The yard had been covered with concrete, and several tons of garbage had to be removed before topsoil could be brought in and the beginnings of the garden laid down.

In designing the twenty-by-forty-foot backyard, the owners (she a fabric painter and he an artist) wanted to expand their living space by creating a room outdoors. They felt a garden would soften

the property and enable them to "walk barefoot in clean grass." Happily, the small yard they have nurtured is more than a romantic sanctuary in a faded industrial neighborhood. By providing privacy, quiet, and extra room in a modest space, this unexpected oasis also offers practical solutions to some typical problems of city living.

A natural extension of the house, the patio functions as a kind of breezy open-air room that takes advantage of its southern exposure to catch sunlight year-round. Its hard-wearing floor, built of old bricks salvaged from the site, makes a physical transition between the house and a grassy yard beyond. With a table and chairs, the terrace

becomes an outdoor dining area, complete with a nearby barbecue.

A formidable barrier, the twenty-three-foot high cinder-block wall at the property's edge was retained to ensure privacy. But to soften it, the owners planted lush Boston ivy, which grows fast and furiously and acts as an effective camouflage and absorbs city sounds. The slower-growing evergreen English ivy provides color throughout winter months. Similarly, a wood trellis entwined with climbing roses adds interest to the rear wall of the house, while vines of Concord grapes and clematis, trained over the portico, shade the patio during summer.

Now, in direct contrast to the concrete and brick surroundings, a blend of color, texture, and fresh scents—even the gentle reflections in the water of the goldfish pond—makes a subtle appeal to all the senses. The mere presence of this neatly landscaped yard, sandwiched improbably between a factory and an abandoned rowhouse, is a surprise and a delight.

Throughout, all of the plants—magnolia and honeysuckle, columbine and potted herbs, foxglove and grapes, ivy and roses—soften and shape the space. The result: a colorful, fragrant, slightly dreamy old-fashioned refuge that proves that any big city can still yield marvelous small wonders.

The ivy tapestry helps muffle city
sounds as it softens the blank
expanse of wall at the garden edge.
A cluster of potted herbs yields
fresh provender for the kitchen,
which returns its scraps to a
compost container at the back of
the yard.

With space at a premium, the
brick barbecue doubles as a potting
table. An old barrel makes a
useful storage bin for charcoal.

Combined with imagination and
a dash of wit, a stone architectural
fragment and wooden plank make
a rustic garden bench alongside
the barbecue.

85

METROPOLITAN HIGH-LIFE

*E*ver since the ancient Mesopotamians devised the world's first urban roof gardens, city dwellers have been fascinated with the idea of reaching skyward for light and views.

The owner of this New York penthouse takes particular pleasure in his four fabulous terraces, where he has nurtured a garden of trees, vines, potted shrubs, and flowers as a lush surprise against the stone and concrete skyline.

Shaped by a clever play of greenery, furnishings, and awnings, this "urban yard" not only offers private, shady alcoves for dining and entertaining but a sky-high refuge from the hectic city below. Well beyond the range of traffic noise, the terraces are exceedingly quiet. Moreover, prevailing breezes and the ample shade from canopies and thick foliage render temperatures a refreshing ten to fifteen degrees cooler than those down on the street. As a result, windows and doors can be left open all summer with no need for air conditioning: an occasional turn of a ceiling fan keeps air circulating.

Varied in size, shape, and location, the rooftop terraces reveal a continually changing panorama of the city skyline. While unified in design by a hard-wearing terrazzo tile, they are physically separate, and each has its own special atmosphere.

Completely secluded and accessible only from the bedroom, the most private is the quiet southern terrace, where a striped awning rolls out to shade a lazy hammock. More public, the remaining spaces open off a glass-and-mirror gallery on the north side. Long, narrow, and lined with potted geraniums and evergreens, the northern terrace functions as a kind of outdoor corridor, inviting visitors to wander and explore. The eastern terrace houses a wonderful cutting garden, roses, vegetables, and herbs. The western terrace, the grandest, is furnished with a massive dining table, lounges and dining chairs, and a canvas canopy, all of which serve a practical purpose in this cool spot for entertaining.

Perhaps most appealing of all the fittings, however, are the wonderful trellis-climbing vines, flowering trees, and vibrant perennials that seem extra-special given their improbable city location. Because strong sun and rooftop winds flatten and dry plants, the owner limits his selection to hardy varieties. Yet the choice, including hydrangeas, wisterias, and weeping mulberries, is surprisingly rich. They do require considerable upkeep—daily watering for at least an hour and a half—but for this gardener it is a fair price for his "piece of the country in the middle of Manhattan."

The private terrace, accessible only through the bedroom, faces south for sunny breakfasts. A cool hammock strung in the shade of a crabapple tree invites late-afternoon lounging.

In the outdoor "corridor," geraniums and impatiens enliven a bland brick facade on one side while ivy softens the parapet opposite. Wonderfully lush, all the terrace plantings require constant watering. To take up overflow, the tile floors have drains.

In the dining area, a new canvas covering put the existing canopy frame back in use. Come winter, the awning is stored indoors. A standard ceiling fan keeps air circulating under the canopy.

The epitome of city sophistication, the west-facing terrace dazzles guests with champagne and spectacular sunsets.

A PERFECT SETTING

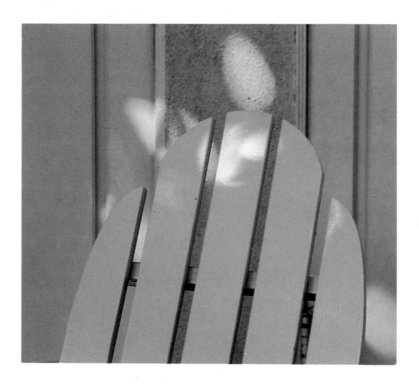

Cool color and hot tropical blossoms were the inspiration for this provocative jungle of a yard that is actually squeezed into a small urban lot but strays miles from civilization in both look and feel. Overflowing with jasmine, shrimp plants, plums, and exotic orchids, the yard provides calm refuge in a populous urban setting. Moreover, it acts as an intriguing link between the owner's streetfront bungalow and the more private, artist's studio she recently built for herself in the back.

Much of this yard's particular appeal lies, in fact, in its careful relationship to the new studio. The work of architects Moore Ruble Yudell, the two were designed for a natural flow between the building—a combination work/living/entertaining space—and the lushly planted area around it.

That important indoor/outdoor transition is largely achieved by the many doors that dissolve boundaries for a feeling of extra space: despite its small size, the seven-hundred-square-foot building has three sets of them. In addition to the more conventional front door, converted garage doors unfold off the studio work space that accommodates typecases and printing equipment, providing instant, natural ventilation. Just around the corner, two pairs of doors can be thrown open to extend the living area directly out to a shady side terrace.

Color and material also play essential roles. Designed with a putty-hued stucco finish and cool blue/gray trim that extend to the garden furnishings, the studio offers a backdrop of muted color that induces an air of restfulness. Paving surfaces combine cement by the studio—for practicality and easy maintenance—and rustic brick for a more romantic look in the entertaining area. And, of course, the dense tangle of tropical greenery contributes to the privacy and quiet as it creates everchanging shadows over this tiny haven.

To expand the living area, glass doors give out to a terrace paved with brick for a rustic look.

Oversized casements frame views of the lush foliage to bring the outdoors inside.

By the studio's front door, a sliced-off building corner is a playful architectural reference to early commercial buildings.

Sixty years old and twenty feet high, a towering magnolia tree provides the main source of shade and creates a tree-house effect in the studio tower.

Planted with a tangle of sage, lobelia, oregano, and peppermint geranium, the corner herb garden is a favorite spot for afternoon reading (overleaf).

COUNTRY

YARDS

SHADY ACRES

With the expansiveness characteristic of an early New England homestead, the yard of this nineteenth-century clapboard residence stretches far beyond the stone-walled boundaries of its trim front lawn. Here it encompasses an entire landscape.

Unfolding behind the spare frame house are five acres of woods, meadows, and pond, woven with the familiar and unmistakable images of a classic New England vista: ribbons of stone wall and picket fence, majestic maple trees, an arbor wound with purple lilacs, a well house, a slate path, a forgotten garden seat. These are indeed the elements that give the property its special character. Yet, added over time, many also play useful, unpretentious roles.

Planted specifically for shade over a hundred years ago, the mature maple trees now help to reduce temperatures significantly during the summer. The shorter yew bushes that camouflage the foundation by the front door, on the other hand, were chosen for the greenery they provide during bleak New England winters.

More recently, the owners used fieldstones found on the property to build a new wall in the front yard. Designed to blend unobtrusively with existing features, the low wall both anchors the house visually in the flat, open front yard and separates it physically from the nearby road.

Still other elements have been preserved and re-used. Relics of a formal garden that once stood behind the house, a stand of lilac and a picket and stone fence now enclose a modern swimming pool that occupies the site. Nearby, a vacant shed has found new life as a storage house for pool and gardening equipment.

To the owners, however, the most essential element of all in their backyard landscape is the pond and its small island. Set behind the house and completely secluded from the road, this natural, spring-fed pond functions as a major feature of landscape design and as a magnet for play and social activities. Cordially shared with a neighbor, the pond is stocked with goldfish, turtles, and catfish. In summer, rowboats float gently across the water, and with the winter freeze, the pond is a stage for skating parties. Light fixtures mounted in the trees above transform it into a dramatic night scene at any time of year. A valued haven for the two families who use it, the pond is a luxury that only a country landscape can offer.

The comfortable chairs are shaded by a century-old maple tree. Behind them is the house's newest addition: a wing with an informal sitting room where the owners enjoy a view of the pond year round.

The view down to the pond embraces a variety of elements: a rustic stone wall in the foreground, a romantic lilac arbor on one side, and a trim patio on the other. In the distance, two Adirondack chairs wait side by side at the water's edge.

A lilac arbor and a picket fence atop a stone wall separate the pool from the lawn.

Classic New England touches include a Colonial-style lantern at the entrance to the driveway and a low stone wall.

With five acres for the children to roam, the family relies on this brass bell to call everyone in for supper. On either side are window boxes filled with pink geraniums that bloom until November, when they are brought inside for the winter.

The owners were able to make use of a number of outbuildings. This storage shed now opens onto the driveway on one side for easy access to the tools stored within.

A COASTAL ALLIANCE

*C*reated amid the rolling dunes and wild grass of a windblown Atlantic beachfront, this is a landscape truly at one with its natural surroundings. Here, in a property where location is everything, the design of house, pool, and deck focuses on a quiet effort to take advantage of the superb views and open-air setting without imposing on them. And while the flow between house and beach may look effortless, that effect is based on an expert understanding of the ecological needs of the property and the subtle tensions that exist between nature and man-made structures.

In an effort to restore the original undulating seaside topography previously flattened when an earlier house was built on site, the designers actually created a new dune by trucking in sand and securing it naturally with a dense cover of beach grass and native shrubs.

On it, they put the house. Around it, they seeded hundreds of hardy, salt-loving plants and trees designed to stabilize the sandy ground plane and provide shelter from prevailing winds. The rich mix of seaside foliage includes only native

Custom cedar planters blend in easily with the pool deck and walls, focusing attention on the deep green junipers they contain.

Overlooking the dunes, the open beach pavilion offers shelter from the relentless sun.

varieties: shore juniper and mungo pine for sturdy ground cover; Japanese black pine, salt spray roses, and highbush blueberries for height and protection. Now, the loose dune plantings on the ocean side blend in seamlessly with the plant growth and a second dune already there.

Similarly, the fir and cedar deck helps tie the pool and house to the wild seascape, while the long boardwalk makes a physical and visual connection to the beach beyond. As an outdoor extension of the house, the generous deck and pool area was designed primarily for entertaining, and can comfortably accommodate several dozen guests. Midway down the boardwalk, an enclosed barbecue area poised amid a protective growth of juniper provides a wonderful interim spot for informal gatherings. It also makes a transition from the fairly "public" walkway to the more private vegetable and herb garden located nearby.

Continuing onward, the boardwalk follows its unerring path to the sea, which, after all, is the ultimate justification for this compelling landscape.

*S*et on a secluded landing in the stairway that continues down to a nearby garden, the barbecue terrace is completely separate from the pool and decks. The grill is made from an old metal oilfield drum. Designed to fit in with natural materials, the gravel floor also absorbs oil and food stains.

*C*utting through a valley between two dunes, the connecting boardwalk makes a smooth transition from deck edge to nature.

*S*et into the beachside end of the boardwalk are a shower nozzle and bench for quick rinses.

*P*lanted with rugged evergreens and salt-loving ground covers designed to protect the sandy dunes from erosion, the windblown landscape stretches out from the house to embrace the sea.

For parties, Adirondack chairs and tables are clustered in small groups, adding spots of interest through the yard. Spare foundation plantings and an uncluttered plan make the yard seem like a spacious open-air room.

Presenting an open, inviting face to the world, the yard is supremely adaptable for entertaining.

SUMMER WHITES

When one Manhattan resident was househunting on Long Island, her priority was to find a sound structure in a convenient location. With the 1845 house she chose came a yard so low-key it could be called a patch of grass. But, far from detrimental, the simple, carefree design is, in fact, the very key to the property's success.

Recognizing that the spare look both suited the older house and could work in her favor, the owner, who is a designer, has interfered with the yard as little as possible, with gratifying results. Her minimal plantings and an open plan not only mean less work, but also create the illusion of far more space than there actually is. Moreover, this refreshingly plain yard makes a clean backdrop for spontaneous, informal entertaining that a more elaborate garden would overwhelm.

Because they are simple and unobtrusive, the few new additions—a fieldstone patio, a tiny herb garden, a summer flower border—seem to fit in naturally, as though they have always been here. As a gardener on a small budget, this new property owner learned that it is sometimes the smallest, least expensive adjustments that actually make the biggest difference. Grass seed scattered on an old

dirt driveway, for instance, not only eliminated an eyesore but enlarged the lawn and sense of space. And by dividing a large forsythia bush into several small ones that could be planted along the property line, she increased privacy with a border at no cost other than labor.

The owner's frequent outdoor parties share the same inventive spirit. Put together on little more than a stylish shoestring, they come together beautifully—and easily—with pretty much whatever is on hand. At a moment's notice, a worn old potting table, spread with a lovely damask cloth, might become a dining table for four. Extra furniture is borrowed from friends—or transplanted right out the door from living room to lawn. That nothing matches is only part of the charm.

What does matter, however, is that friends feel comfortable and relaxed. To this end, small islands of chairs and tables are casually set around the yard to encourage guests to wander and explore, choosing shade, sun, and conversation as they please. Similarly, summer meals of farmstand fare are served in casual buffets that are savored as much for their pretty presentation as their cool summer flavors.

A delicate accent against dove gray shingles, the potted rose doubles as a versatile decorative device: picked up and moved, it instantly dresses up any part of the yard.

*T*he key to high-style, low-budget entertaining: imagination. From roadside to pitcher, a clutch of wildflowers becomes a charming country bouquet. Borrowed chairs gain new life with a quick cover-up for seats, while the striped tablecloth is run up in minutes on the sewing machine. Just a convenient step or two from the kitchen door, a small table is set for bar duty. Extras that make a difference without stretching the budget are a tin washtub cooler, secondhand baskets, and a potted hydrangea.

*P*ut together an evening or two beforehand, a dozen tarts will feed seventy guests. Some sweet, some savory, these summer tarts are luscious combinations of fresh local farm produce.

*A*n expanse of open lawn is the ideal playground for favorite games such as croquet.

114

THE SHADES OF SUMMER

As part-time residents, vacation-house owners often opt for distinctly seasonal gardens and yards that peak during just a few short weeks of the year. When designing a new yard for an old cottage near the seashore, the owner of this weekend hideaway concentrated his efforts on creating garden color between June and August, the months when he is most apt to be there to enjoy it.

Because he wanted a meticulous landscape marked by careful grooming, the owner chose a formal composition for the three-quarter-acre yard, and relies on a professional gardener to keep it in good condition. Hidden by tall pruned hedges on one side and a dense growth of trees on the other, the yard can be entered only from the house or by an arbor gateway off the drive. The effect is one of total privacy that contrives to heighten the expectation that something special awaits within.

It does. Arranged around an unbroken expanse of manicured lawn from which the owner even removed such intrusions as old stone paths, the secluded yard spreads out from a central, circular bed of cutting flowers. This easy, flowing design encompasses such small delights as a tranquil gold-fish pond and a shady terrace tucked into a grove of greenery and iris.

The real focus of this garden, however, is the intense color contrast created by a wide variety of flowers blooming against the uninterrupted verdant background of hedges and lawn. In June, there is the spectacular orange of poppies and the brilliant white of iris. Later months bring deep, satisfying pink tea roses, followed by blue alliums and yellow honeysuckle. Later still, Concord grapes ripen into a robust burst of purple. These plants thrive in the moist seaside climate.

Amid this indulgent mix of fruit and flowers there are a few carefully placed objects. At the center of the circular bed, a bronze astrolabe, an ancient device used to determine the position of celestial bodies, acts as an architectural anchor. Chippendale-style planters flank an old overgrown arbor that forms the private entry from the driveway. While on the brick terrace, a pair of bronze Oriental dogs act as silent guards. Subtle but important, these details introduce a more personal element to the garden and contribute to an overall effect that is formal, yet very inviting.

A burst of intense orange against the dark green backdrop, the poppies are early summer bloomers that thrive in the damp seaside climate.

Sculpted into a gentle curve over the entrance, a tall, trimmed privet hedge screens the yard from the driveway. By training the hedge over an old arbor salvaged from a nearby house, the owner created an unusually private entry, flanked by potted yews for formal symmetry.

117

Lush expanses of lawn and foliage serve only to enhance the intense colors of the flowers. Here a deep red peony blooms against a background of trimmed lawn.

Bricks are laid in a classic basketweave pattern on the terrace where a white Lutyens bench stands.

In spring, iris and poppies bloom around the astrolabe.

Blooming with poppies, peonies, and iris, the circular flower bed forms a central focus for the yard. The fragrant pink tea roses, foreground, are for cutting.

Behind a rustic bench, the old potting shed is grown over with ivy to make it more a part of the yard architecture.

118

VICTORIAN COUNTERPOINT

*O*ld-fashioned American vacation cottages are wonderfully appealing precisely because they were designed for comfortable summer living. Originally part of an old Methodist camp community, the two breezy, rambling Victorians here couldn't be better equipped for warm weather and the easy way of life it brings.

The essence of these neighboring houses is found in their enormous, glorious porches. There are downstairs verandas and upstairs sleeping porches, side porches, and back porches in both houses. Even some of the rooms, with their windows on three sides for natural ventilation, resemble porches.

Because he felt the right look for the front porch was so important, the current owner of this 1875 house took particular care to restore the elaborate gingerbread trim that is its distinguishing mark. When he purchased the house, only a tiny bit of the original jigsaw detailing survived on a railing. An exact reproduction of the ornate, often three-dimensional designs would have been

prohibitively expensive. But by examining old photographs and looking at other period houses in the neighborhood, he was able to recapture the right look by designing a simpler replacement that nevertheless is in complete harmony with the house. Made from sturdy marine plywood, this "modern" gingerbread proved a less costly alternative, and should hold up to the elements for years.

Because life in the Methodist camp focused on communal activities away from the house, much of the half-acre yard itself has only been developed relatively recently, and is still by and large an easy, carefree place. Its particular charm lies in its informality and a slightly, although highly suitable, unkempt look.

Outside, in the deep shade of enormous oak trees, everything seems to grow and wander almost on its own. Designing the garden himself, the owner deliberately chose old-fashioned flowers that match the nostalgic feel of the house and need little care. In one spot, lilies and hollyhocks

The yuard draws particular
interest from its variety of seating
areas. Painted Adirondack chairs
and cushioned lounge chairs are
perfect for chatting, sunning,
or reading.

The Victorian front gate, set
amid lilies and junipers, was
bought by the owner at a local
antique shop. It suited perfectly,
he felt, the "slight folly feel" of
the house.

The shady, open porch is a cool refuge from intense summer sun or sudden showers. All thrift shop finds, the wicker, bamboo, and wood furniture is unified with dark green paint.

sprawl around a picket fence; in another, roses climb over an old arbor that has been placed as a focal point at the end of the property.

Staggered for continuous blooming, the perennials fill beds bordered by shade-loving impatiens to guarantee color from June to the first frost. And everywhere, there are lovely places to sit with a book or with nothing at all to do—a wrought-iron bench amid the flowers, Adirondack porch chairs planted in a bed of ivy, a lazy hammock strung between two trees. "It's all part of a neighborly feel," says the owner, who finds it the ideal setting for the ideal summer house.

A picket fence along one side of the property is softened by sprawling roses and mixed perennials. This romantic border requires little upkeep for the owner, who likes to think of himself " as a weeder, not a gardener." At the far corner of the property an arbor provides a vanishing point where path and fence meet. Put in quite recently, it might, by looks, have been there forever.

The view from the sleeping porch to the house across the street captures the appealing neighborly feel that exists between the two old properties.

VICTORIAN COUNTERPOINT

*E*asy summer living continues across the street. The owners of this nineteenth-century house were attracted by its open, airy feel. Now they spend much of their time on the expansive wraparound porch, where each section, furnished for a slightly different purpose, is an outdoor room.

To preserve the original character of both house and yard, the family has kept changes to a minimum over the years, choosing to make the most of what was already there. Removing some large cedar trees in front made a dramatic difference to the porch by opening it up to sunlight and breezes, and also effectively thwarted the roof-bound raccoons who were using the branches as ladders. With the help of friends, the owners were able to rescue an old tennis court from a snarl of weeds behind the house.

The rest of the yard was left as open lawn with the old oaks, firs, and apple trees that give the property its wonderfully shady, summery feeling. Because they are not serious gardeners, the owners preferred to leave the yard in its rambling state, which was perfectly suited to the house itself. There is a small vegetable garden stocked with summer fare—fragrant herbs and tomatoes—by the kitchen door. Flowers are hardy perennials and bulbs such as lilies, which can be planted and then largely forgotten.

Otherwise, life goes on the way it always has in this sleepy old summer house, where even the linens are still hung out to dry the way they should be—in the fresh air and sunshine.

In the northeast corner of the porch a rope hammock catches the early sun.

*M*ore social moments are spent on the opposite porch, whose antique rope furniture came with the house. Also found in the house, 1930s tennis rackets are a nostalgic reminder of games past.

*T*en-speed bicycles look inconspicuous stored on the porch, proving that this house is not just a period piece.

*S*alvaged from years of neglect, the tennis court was refurbished. Primroses and day lilies border the path to the court. A wooden park bench in the shade of a maple tree provides a cool vantage point.

A more practical inheritance is the clothesline outside the kitchen door. Hung up to dry in the sun, the antique linens that were found in the house rarely need to be bleached or ironed.

On the porch, the wicker chaise, which dates from the 1920s, epitomizes the gracefulness of the old house.

FARM FOLLOWS FUNCTION

Wide open spaces and controlled formality shaped the aesthetic master plan for this complex of white nineteenth-century farm buildings, recently renovated by architect Raymond Gomez and Mariette Himes Gomez, an interior designer, as their year-round weekend retreat.

And indeed, a master plan was in order, for when the owners purchased the former barnyard a few years ago, they found nothing much more than a rundown jumble of sheds, stables, and barns. But by rebuilding some and moving others, they instilled the old property with new life and sophistication without compromising the openness and rural simplicity that was its initial attraction.

Throughout the grounds, century-old oaks and linden trees were preserved for their scale, wonderful shade, and feeling of timeless stability. The new hedges and wood slat fences added around the property provide privacy and help define areas.

In contrast with the expansive lawns, the varied outbuildings—a well house, outhouse, granary, goat shed, and a new garage—create a nest of intimate spaces close to the house, itself renovated from two adjacent barns and a connecting stable.

At center, slipped between the well house and the old granary, is the new swimming pool, which, as the main summer living space, was conceived as an important and integral part of the landscape. Designed with a black lining to make it look deeper, the pool appears to sink naturally into the bluestone terrace that connects it to the house and lawn. Moreover, its attenuated dimensions—it is one foot narrower than the standard twenty feet—also make it seem much longer than it actually is, and help draw the eye out and away from the house to the open lawn beyond.

Across the flat property, a fresh coat of white paint on fence, house, and outbuildings alike unifies these once disparate elements with a rustic simplicity and light formality. In turn, plantings of ivy, boxwood, ferns, and small spreading junipers make a cool, deliberate counterpoint of green that the designers extended to even such small details as the canvas on the poolside deck chairs. This strong network of repeated colors works throughout the landscape, giving a pleasing sense of continuity to an old property that has clearly embraced its new use.

Classic striped canvas deck chairs are light enough to be moved about the poolside. Behind them, a tall board fence in the farmyard vernacular helps provide privacy.

Located only twenty-two feet from the house, the elongated pool becomes a major element in the landscape design. The black rubberized liner keeps the water ten degrees warmer by soaking up sunlight.

*A*n old well house still holds the well, but it also holds new pool equipment. Because the shed is right next to the pool, summer paraphernalia can be quickly stored out of sight at the end of the day. The birdhouse is one of dozens collected by Raymond Gomez that can be seen on every building on the property.

*I*ts clean, classic design blends the new garage with older surrounding farm buildings. The sandy driveway will eventually be paved with crushed stone.

The complex of house, fences, and small outbuildings is arranged to create a succession of inviting, well-defined spaces near the house. The gate opens off the parking area.

Nestled under an awning of trees, a pair of Adirondack chairs, a birdhouse, and a simply planted urn reflect the owners' attention to detail. Set at the base of several trees, outdoor lights provide nighttime drama.

JUST REWARDS

When asked to describe the most beautiful sight she could imagine, Virginia Woolf once responded: "Sunlight on leaves." The owners of this sleek weekend retreat must feel the same way, for it was the woods that first drew them to their hillside property near the Atlantic seacoast.

Designed by architect Harry Bates around a transplanted 1789 barn, the house has a clean, simple look that does not disturb the natural beauty of the wild scrub oaks, rhododendrons, and laurels. Quietly embracing the slanting site, its yard relies on a skillful weaving of plantings, decks, and boardwalks to orchestrate the changing levels visually while creating areas of total privacy within.

Inside the house, sliding glass doors make an effortless flow from the warm, rustic interior to the cool views of woods and ocean beyond. Outside, the intriguing play of decks, paths, and walls entices the visitor down steps and around corners into sun-dappled terraces and shady, vine-entwined alcoves.

While some areas are physically connected, others are quite separate and apart. Thus the purely functional driveway and parking area are located in front, but are not looked onto from the house or the rest of the property.

Equally secluded, the swimming pool is hidden below and in back, out of sight of both house and driveway. A dense growth of rhododendron, holly, and white azalea provides color and protection, and is an attractive pool screen on even the darkest days of winter.

To avoid the bare look of many contemporary houses, the owners left existing trees in place wherever possible, then filled in with hardy evergreens and ivy. They also resisted small plants and flowers to avoid clutter and preserve the clarity of the overall design.

For the wonderfully natural front yard, the existing scrub oaks were cleaned up, cleared, and pruned selectively to open the area and bring in enough sunlight to grow grass. The result is a thoroughly unusual, appealing expanse of lawn that, spiked at random with slender tree trunks, resembles a kind of enigmatic miniature forest. And although they need frequent pruning, it is well worth it for the owners, who spend as much time as possible outdoors enjoying their yard.

*T*he sculptural quality of the front yard is a result of trimming off scrub oak branches as high as fifteen feet. Here, in springtime, over a thousand daffodils bloom.

*T*o minimize intrusions, the parking area is located out of sight of the rest of the yard. Scattered across the grass, random flagstones make an informal, natural path.

*D*esigned to integrate the various grade levels, cedar decks and pathways were kept as sleek and simple as possible to blend in with natural surroundings. The pressure-treated wood requires minimal upkeep.

*B*ehind the secluded pool, rhododendrons, azaleas, and holly were planted for sequential blooming. A dark pool liner keeps the look natural and pondlike.

A consistent use of weathered wood helps unify the deck, walkways, and house: even the pool furniture is custom-colored to blend in easily.

*A*t the side of the house, a vine-entwined pergola makes a shady dining spot. Made of decking material to match, the cedar table and chairs were designed by the architect specifically for the space.

*P*laying off barn forms, a silo-like deck shelters outside access to the master bath. Glass doors from the indoor shower open directly onto the enclosed deck.

PORTRAIT OF A GARDEN

Originally a farmhouse, this nineteenth-century homestead tucked amid the remnants of an old pear orchard has taken on a new life as the relaxed, informal setting for a weekend residence and studio. Like the 1895 house, which has been enlarged and modified over the years, the yard is a simple, lighthearted place. The hand of the owner, a painter and botanical illustrator, is visible everywhere in the sensitive combination of color and texture. Flower beds, planted with a personal selection of delicate pastels, meld into open fields and give way to grassy paths. Even formal hedges coexist with overgrown weeds for a natural effect.

Deceptive in its simplicity, however, that harmony belies the careful consideration that shapes the house and its relationship to the grounds. Because the flowers are both the inspiration and the subject for his paintings, the owner placed each bed so that they can be seen from the house and studio.

Trees were used to screen and shade, and a tall hedge blocks off the view of the driveway and any cars that might be parked there. In front of the house, a bed of bleached gravel helps link structure to yard by creating a courtyard effect. A durable surface for heavy traffic, the pale stone also has the unexpected benefit of reflecting additional light into the house and studio.

For his garden, the painter, who picks his flowers for their colors and interesting shapes, created a deliberately pale palette of pinks, blues, yellows, and white with a mix of perennials that includes foxgloves, clematis, peonies, roses, buddleia, and purple allium. Although the existing clay-based

soil had been fine for the former fruit orchard, it was necessary to supplement it with fresh topsoil to support the flowers and hemlocks that were planted as part of the new landscape design.

The traditional flowers, together with a dozen or so pear trees from the old orchard, define a series of walkways and outdoor "rooms" that spread out from the house. The most formal is an oval garden, which the owner enclosed with a curved hemlock hedge. From the outside, this "secret" garden can be glimpsed only through four small openings spaced at even intervals. These partial views consciously imply a greater space, and even a bit of mystery, beyond. Inside, the feeling is of seclusion and calm.

*T*all varieties such as foxgloves and purple allium define the gravel courtyard boundaries. Just outside the studio door, a white iceberg rose blooms for several weeks each summer.

*M*uch of the property is left to grow wild, but in certain places the grass is trimmed to create informal seating areas. The highest point facing west is bathed in late-afternoon sun, and commands a view to distant mountains.

*T*ucked into the delicate pastels, more robust shades refresh the eye. Here the pinks of foxgloves, alliums, and miniature carnations are displayed against the vivid blue background of delphinium.

*M*asses of peonies, lavender, and delphinium thrive in the shelter of a hemlock hedge.

*W*here appropriate, flowers have been chosen to add to the informal mood. Roses, usually old-fashioned varieties, are allowed to ramble and climb.

*V*irtually in a room of its own, the summer tea table is enveloped by high hedges. The umbrella, though stabilized by a heavy base, is still light enough to be moved around the yard.

AMERICAN COUNTRY
AT HOME

A well-known authority on folk art and Americana, Mary Emmerling is long familiar with the inherent simplicity and warmth of the look known as "American Country." It seems only logical, then, that those same qualities shape her own country house, an informal, easy-care retreat designed for herself and her two children.

Only recently completed, the expansive shingle-and-clapboard vacation house already looks comfortably settled into the seaside landscape. And just as the building borrows its spare lines and traditional details from older farmhouses in this region of flat, rural potato fields, the open yard takes its cue from familiar farmyard images of picket fence and dooryard garden.

Extremely simple and bare of intrusions—even the swimming pool is cut cleanly into the ground—the one-acre property and the house were conceived as a succession of places "where people can go off by themselves." Of these, perhaps the favorite is the spacious, old-fashioned screened porch that

opens off the living room. Not only does this extra room provide a cool, bug-free spot for reading, conversation, and dining all summer long, but it means doors to the house proper can stay open, even on rainy days.

Outside, the yard breaks into a series of inviting areas designed to catch the changing sunlight as the day goes on. A rustic table and chairs set out by the pool, for instance, make an ideal spot for summer lunches. The small flagstone terrace off

the living room is the favored place for afternoon tea, while the nearby side yard is the chosen badminton court.

Still, easy summer living needn't be without celebration. For the ultimate American Country holiday—the Fourth of July—the decorations are appropriately simple. Waving American flags and pieces from her folk art collection are found around the house and yard as evidence of Mary Emmerling's warm, down-to-earth style.

At the front door, a picket fence creates a yard within a yard to recall traditional dooryard gardens.

French doors in the living room allow fragrant, cool sea breezes to drift inside.

The hand-stitched folk art flag adds a touch of whimsy to the classic nine-paned door.

Rabbits are kept out of the herb garden by low picket fence.

*M*ismatched chairs and antique wicker make comfortable furnishings for the screened porch. An old drysink has been promoted to a bar, while the doorside wicker basket makes a convenient catchall for hockey sticks, baseball bats, and an umbrella.

*A*n old granite-ware pitcher holds snapdragons with country style.

A swinging, barn-like door helps an outdoor shower blend in with the shingle house. The weathered towel rack and bench winter outdoors.

Freshly sodded, the flat yard can be the setting for games of croquet, soccer, or badminton.

Built of plain wood boards, the peak-roofed storage shed was designed to have the same lines as the house.

DESIGN FOR LIVING

For interior designer Christine Maly, the secluded creekside location and superb views around her tiny one-room cottage have always been a greater incentive to be outside than in one room. So, when she decided to expand the former boathouse with extra living space, she chose to add on where she would use it most: outdoors.

With a simple pine deck and a few easy furnishings, Maly completely transfigured the little house by creating what amounts to three open-air summertime rooms. Moreover, as she is handy with hammer and saw, the designer was able to keep costs down by designing the deck and building most of it herself. With help from family members, it took just a few weekends to complete.

Simply constructed of stock-sized pressure-treated pine straight from the lumberyard, the platform deck bases its pleasing, compact design on a pattern of thirty-inch-square modules that play off the dimensions of the house itself. The original idea was to move the modules around for a continuously changing design. The swelling and shrinking caused by damp sea air, however, eventually required that they be nailed permanently in place.

Even so, the deck seems perfectly right, neither interfering with the natural landscape nor overpowering the modest house. Raised off the ground-plane, it is not only practical for its flood-prone location, but adds some design interest where frequently rising waters rule out any kind of garden or permanent planting.

Its appeal lies in a simple, zizagging plan that skirts the house and then skews out into the lawn, incorporating three connected but different areas along the way: a waterside dining room, a sun deck, and, catercorner to the southwest, a hammock strung in the shade of an old linden tree.

Even the furnishings reflect Maly's personal and resourceful touch. A mix of yard-sale finds and weekend handiwork, they suit an easygoing look that combines the best of two worlds: high style and low maintenance.

The middle deck is given over to sunbathing. Lounges were made from leftover lumber, then padded with canvas cushions. The cushions quickly roll up for storage inside during the week, when the owner is away.

Strung between the fences, under an old linden tree, the hammock is furnished with an oversize pillow and a relaxed cat.

Just a few feet from the water, the dining deck is sunny throughout the day. Because the yard is vulnerable to rising waters, plants are limited to potted varieties such as the foxgloves at the side of the house.

Utterly simple and completely open, the deck becomes an ever-changing stage.

157

THEIR NEW HOMESTEAD

When landscape gardener Lisa Stamm and her husband, Dale Booher, an architect, purchased this two-hundred-year-old cottage they literally found themselves living with little more than a roof over their heads. There was no electricity on the old sea captain's property, and the only plumbing was an old hand pump and two outhouses. But what began ten years ago as a tiny weekend getaway on a featureless acre and a half has expanded into a full-time residence and landscape business. With its intriguing mix of cool lawn, bright flowers, and unexpected tangle of woods, it is a wonderful illustration of how something exceptional can emerge from humble beginnings.

Much of the design's success comes from the skillful integration of different elements. The most functional are located at the entrance, screened by a tall fence and hedge from the house. Here, the gravel driveway offers parking space for cars and landscaping equipment and storage for potted plants that await delivery. To one side a vegetable gar-

*T*he center of activity in the property is the pool, whose gray gunite lining vividly reflects surrounding trees and roses. The cabana, curtained and cushioned and trimmed whimsically with small brass tassels, is a romantic retreat.

den includes tomatoes, asparagus, peppers, and tall raspberry canes.

A small gate in the neat hedge invites visitors into the more private yard proper, to find a confident mix of formal and informal. On this side, the tall privet forms a stately backdrop to a perennial bed of fat hybrid lilies, larkspurs, allium, and Shasta daisies, edged by an old-fashioned stone wall. The easy look belies the care this bed requires: Stamm hoses it daily during hot weather, believing that "you don't know your plants if you don't water them by hand." An exquisite Belgian espalier of interwoven pear and apple trees, on the other hand, is less work than it looks: quick pruning three times each summer keeps the trees in shape.

The yard itself focuses on the swimming pool, which is surrounded by a brilliant display of roses through most of the summer. On one side is a snug cabana, rebuilt with new trellis walls from a shed found on the property. On a more practical note, the owners have installed a removable fence of two-by-fours and wire net around the pool area as a safety precaution for their young daughter, Vanessa.

In recent years, the owners have been able to protect their privacy by joining with a neighbor to purchase twelve acres of adjoining woodland, including a large pond. Still wild, these outlying woods make a romantic contrast to the ordered flower beds and trimmed lawn of the original property.

For the future, Stamm and Booher plan more landscaping in the woods. Now, only an old statue, nearly lost amid ivy and ferns, is a suggestion that more is to come.

From the gravel driveway, one can see two very different entrances to the property. The small wood gate set in a tall trimmed privet hedge barely hints at the expansive property beyond. On either side, a pair of potted marguerites are a formal note.

At the service entrance, lattice gates open wide to allow access for trucks and heavy landscaping equipment. Closed, they blend quietly into the hedge.

*W*here possible, old structures
on the property were preserved and
adapted to the owner's needs. At
the end of a long bed of perennials,
two old sheds now form storage
for garden tools and a croquet set.

*S*trung between two trees near
the front of the house, a double
rope hammock is generous enough
to accommodate two friends.

*U*ntamed, the woods surrounding
the property are extra privacy
for the house and yard (overleaf).

DESIGN

DETAILS

GATES AND FENCES

Gateways frequently shape our first impressions of a property. Here, two rustic white gates at country houses are contrasted with a more elaborate arched trellis crowned with lilac.

Vines, shrubs and trees can be trained to soften the lines of a fence, increase privacy, or even form the fence itself. At top, pear and apple trees have been trained and intertwined in a Belgian espalier to form a living fence. Below, dozens of iris, foxgloves, and other flowers soften chain link; a stand of mature trees has been pruned to suggest a wall.

167

FENCES

Roses and other garden plants are allowed to ramble and overwhelm this traditional picket fence around a country yard, opposite top. A tree mimics its surrounding wood-slat fence while tall hedges, opposite bottom, reinforce a simple post-and-rail fence. Dry stone walls add a traditional touch even as retaining walls and can be combined effectively with wood lattice or picket, top and center, for added height.

PATHS

Paths lead the eye, define boundaries, and separate different areas in a yard as well as provide hard-wearing traffic areas. The warm tones of brick, left, will create a rustic, informal feeling. Gravel or slabs of fieldstone laid in a crazy-paving pattern achieve the same effect, this page bottom right and center, especially when softened by low-growing plants. Log sections match the country look of the gateway, right; terracotta tiles, here enlivened with colored

insets, are a more formal and practical choice for heavy-use areas; diverging, regularly spaced stone slabs draw strong abstract lines across a lawn. Neutral-toned wood, used on decks and pool surrounds, can extend into a yard as a durable walkway.

SEATING

Traditional garden furniture in stone, wood, or metal blends quickly and naturally into its setting. The two metal benches shown here represent the classical, below, and the ornate, in the cast-iron Victorian seat, top left.

The Lutyens bench, opposite center, has more formal lines. Outdoor seating in rustic regional styles is of unfinished wood or twigs. Opposite right, an Adirondack chair is given a contemporary look with a bright coat of paint.

SEATING

Modern garden furniture comes in a variety of durable, easy-care materials. The lounge and chairs in these two sitting areas are made of lightweight tubular metal with a plastic or water-resistant paint finish. On the opposite page, a metal rocker waits poolside and an English park bench provides seating for late-afternoon tea.

ANIMALS

It is only natural that animals should abound in a yard, even in the middle of a city. Here, a menagerie of birds, beasts, and fowl add a witty touch to anything from a faucet to a flagpole.

ORNAMENTS

A yard can be home to a diversity of objects and structures. Stone architectural fragments and sculpture, below, and more formal garden ornaments such as the stone finial opposite enliven and add interest to a property. Bird houses are more practical architectural additions. Easily installed in a screen, a pet door ensures that the yard can be home to a cat or dog all day.

CONTAINERS

Around the yard, containers serve a multitude of purposes, from the ad hoc mailbox, bottom right, to carrying cuttings or fresh flowers in from the garden. Formal permanent planters of almost any size can be made from wood lined with a waterproof material, below. Traditional terracotta is still the preferred choice for most containers. For a display of kitchen herbs and flowers, a movable wire stand, right, will hold a dozen clay pots at once.

BACKYARD

DESIGN

CATALOG

*The following is a selection of some of the best sources of items
for the backyard, including general and specialist
plant and seed suppliers. All of those listed will sell through
the mail and all, except for the antiques stores, will
send a mail-order catalog on request. Because the stock in the
antiques stores varies, they recommend that you call
or write with a description of the kind of item you want.*

GENERAL CATALOGS

Abercrombie & Fitch
Mailing List Preference Service
P.O. Box 70858
Houston, TX 77270

The classic catalog, with pool floats, deck chairs, wicker picnic baskets, and equipment for such backyard games as croquet, horseshoes, miniature golf, and volleyball.

Brookstone Company
127 Vose Farm Road
Peterborough, NH 03458

A general catalog that includes garden tools, sundials, furniture, flags, swings, a Pawley's Island hammock, and a hammock stand.

Clapper's
1125 Washington Street
West Newton, MA 02165

Classic American and English wood furniture, a wide variety of well-made handtools, waterproof planters, and outdoor lighting sets.

Gardener's Eden
P.O. Box 7307
San Francisco, CA 94120

Rustic furniture, trellises and arbors, various planters, and a good variety of garden ornaments.

Gardener's Supply Company
128 Intervale Road
Burlington, VT 05401

A serious gardener's catalog offering items such as plastic cold frames, compostors, tillers, and irrigation systems.

Hammacher Schlemmer
147 East 57th Street
New York, NY 10022

The unusual and hard-to-find: folding portable grills, solar-powered outdoor lights, motorized wheelbarrows, infrared security lights, pool games, and outdoor speakers.

The Kinsman Company
River Road
Point Pleasant, PA 18950

Unpretentious catalog of tools and accessories for the serious gardener including plant supports, tools, watering cans, cold frames, compost bins, arbors and arches.

The Nature Company
P.O. Box 2310
Berkeley, CA 94702

General catalog includes stone birdbaths, Soleri Bells, sundials, bird feeders, and giant, inflatable animals suitable for pool use.

The Plow and Hearth
560 Main Street
Madison, VA 22727

Green River garden tools, various birdhouses, birdbaths, and bird feeders, and outdoor furniture covers.

Renovator's Supply
Millers Falls, MA 01349

Reproductions of Victorian hardware and accessories, including spigots, sundials, lights, birdhouses, and weathervanes.

Smith and Hawken
25 Corte Madera
Mill Valley, CA 94941

English and Japanese garden tools, irrigation and sprinkler systems, classic wood furniture, and planters of fiberglass and plastic.

Walpole Woodworkers
767 East Street
Walpole, MA 02081

Rustic cedar furniture, including swings and picnic sets, cabanas and other small buildings, and a wide range of accessories from weathervanes to mailboxes.

Winterthur Museum and Gardens
Winterthur, DE 19735

A general gift catalog that offers a good variety of planters and a select listing of rare shrubs and trees from the Winterthur Gardens.

Wolfman-Gold & Good Company
484 Broome Street
New York, NY 10013

Planters, latticework window boxes, statuary, gardening tools, a variety of picnic baskets, garden furniture and umbrellas, and doormats.

ANTIQUES

Crowther of Syon Lodge
Syon Lodge
Busch Corner
London Road
Isleworth, Middlesex TW7 SBH
England

A one-hundred-year-old family business that sells antique ornaments and architectural details for house and garden. An extraordinary collection, including some very fine antiques.

Irreplaceable Artifacts
14 Second Avenue
New York, NY 10003

Authentic stone benches, friezes, statuary, usually one-of-a-kind.

Lost City Arts
339 Bleecker Street
New York, NY 10014

Extensive collection of antique accessories for the garden: urns, columns, furniture, cast-iron fences, lamps, friezes, weathervanes.

Urban Archaeology
137 Spring Street
New York, NY 10012

Antique statuary, furniture, ornaments in stone, iron, and terracotta.

ARCHITECTURAL DETAILS AND ORNAMENTS

Cape Cod Cupola
78 State Road, Route 6
North Dartmouth, MA 02747

Hundreds of traditional, handmade aluminum and copper weathervanes, as well as cupolas, wall eagles, mailbox signs, weather stations, and bird feeders.

Cumberland Woodcraft Company, Inc.
P.O. Drawer 609
Carlisle, PA 17013

Hardwood standard and custom corbels, capitals, gables, and architectural trim, as well as complete gazebos in Victorian patterns.

Florentine Craftsmen
46-224 28th Street
Long Island City, NY 11101

*Ornamental metalwork, including complete fountains,
statues, birdbaths, astrolabes, sundials, and urns.*

Gazebo and Porchworks
3901 North Meridian
Puyallup, WA 98371

*Wood rose-arbor kit, covered arbor with swing, porch
swing, gingerbread, and turned columns.*

Haas Wood and Ivory Works, Inc.
64 Clementina Street
San Francisco, CA 94105

*One-hundred-year-old firm specializing in custom and
stock wood trim, brackets, and columns; can work from
client's drawings.*

Kenneth Lynch & Sons
P.O. Box 488
Wilton, CT 06897

*Extensive range of fountains and pools, statuary, gates,
planters, benches, finials, and sundials.*

Moultrie Manufacturing Company
P.O. Drawer 1179
Moultrie, GA 31776

*Cast-aluminum columns with various capitals and bases,
both standard and custom.*

Robinson Iron
P.O. Box 1119
Alexander City, AL 35010

*Cast-iron fountains, statuary, furniture, posts, and
finials.*

Steptoe and Wife Antiques, Ltd.
3626 Victoria Park Avenue
Willowdale, Ontario M2H 3B2
Canada

*Reproduction cast-iron regular and circular staircases and
table bases in Victorian styles, as well as marble
tabletops.*

Worthington Group, Ltd.
P.O. Box 53101
Atlanta, GA 30355

*Pine pedestals in a variety of finishes and columns and
capitals in assorted sizes and styles.*

Vintage Woodworks
Box 1157
513 South Adams
Fredericksburg, TX 78624

*Victorian and country gingerbread pine trim and a
Victorian-style gazebo.*

BARBECUES AND GRILLS

Barbecues Galore
14048 East Firestone Boulevard
Santa Fe Springs, CA 90670

*Extensive choice of smokers and gas, charcoal, electric,
and infrared barbecues, as well as accessories.*

Brookstone Company
127 Vose Farm Road
Peterborough, NH 03458

Barbecues and barbecue cooking equipment.

Chef's Catalog
3215 Commercial Avenue
Northbrook, IL 60062

Selection of barbecues, smokers, and grills, equipment, and mesquite chips.

Cook'n Cajun
P.O. Box 3726
Shreveport, LA 71133

Water smokers and grills in a variety of sizes.

Grillworks, Inc.
1211 Ferdon Road
Ann Arbor, MI 48104

Manufacturer of movable, wood-fueled rotisserie/grills.

BIRDHOUSES AND FEEDERS

Duncraft
Penacook, NH 03303

Specialist feeder, bath, house, and feed supply source, with houses designed just for purple martins.

Hyde Bird Feeder Company
P.O. Box 168
Waltham, MA 02254

Hummingbird feeders, hanging and post feeders, and window feeders.

The Plow and Hearth
560 Main Street
Madison, VA 22727

Various baths, feeders, and houses in concrete, aluminum, and wood, including a house that can be raised and lowered on a high pole.

Wild Bird Supplies
4815 Oak Street
Crystal Lake, IL 60012

Almost everything for the bird-lover: bird houses, feeders, feed, books, and records.

Wolfman-Gold & Good Company
484 Broome Street
New York, NY 10013

Elaborate birdhouses in a number of architectural styles such as Greek Revival and Mission Church, as well as a special house for martins.

CHILDREN'S PLAY EQUIPMENT

Childlife Play Specialties, Inc.
P.O. Box 527
Holliston, MA 01746

Modular wood jungle gyms, swings, slides, treehouses, playhouses, and sandboxes.

Hearth Song
P.O. Box B
Sebastopol, CA 95472

Various old-fashioned children's toys and games, including a gym set, playhouse, windchimes, and picnic hamper.

Walpole Woodworkers
767 East Street
Walpole, MA 02081

Jungle gyms, sandboxes, and furniture made of cedar, as well as freestanding wood playhouses.

Woodplay
P.O. Box 27904
Raleigh, NC 27611

Modular redwood jungle gyms, seesaws, tree houses with swings, and swing and slide sets.

FURNITURE AND PLANTERS

Amish Outlet
Box 102, RD 1
New Wilmington, PA 16142

Bent hickory and plain oak furniture, all handcrafted by the Amish.

BenchCraft
36 New Port Drive
Wayne, PA 19087

Cast-aluminum tables and chairs, some in ornate Victorian designs; English teak chairs, tables, and lounges, including white Lutyens benches.

Cape Cod Comfys
P.O. Box 15103
Seattle, WA 98115

West Coast source of unfinished Adirondack chairs in pine or cedar, as well as porch swings.

Country Casual
17317 Germantown Road
Germantown, MD 20874

Mostly English-designed and manufactured tables, chairs, benches, swings, and planters in teak, including classic English benches.

Country Loft
South Shore Park
Hingham, MA 02043

Rope hammocks.

The Greenery
3237 Pierce Street
San Francisco, CA 94123

Artisan-carved redwood furniture washed with cement to look sun-bleached: benches, chairs, lounges, and tables.

La Lune Collection
241 North Broadway
Milwaukee, WI 53202

Bent-willow chaises, tables, and sofas with canvas cushions.

Lister Teak, Inc.
561 Exton Commons
Exton, PA 19341

Traditional English teak tables, chairs, benches, and planters, all imported.

Daniel Mack Rustic Furnishings
507 West 125th Street
New York, NY 10025

Imaginative twig furniture, each piece made to order and one-of-a-kind.

Moultrie Manufacturing Co.
P.O. Drawer 1179
Moultrie, GA 31768

Cast-aluminum reproductions of Victorian and Old South chairs, tables, settees, and planters.

The Rocker Shop
P.O. Box 12
Marietta, GA 30061

Traditional hand-caned wood rocking chairs and footstools, porch swings, and side tables.

Santa Barbara Designs
205 West Carillo Street
Santa Barbara, CA 93101

Collapsible furniture and umbrellas made of oak, mahogany, (custom) teak, with colorful fabrics.

Settona Willow Company
41655 Magnolia
Murietta, CA 92362

Traditional bent willow furniture for house or garden, also rustic bent willow gates and fences made-to-order.

Shaker Workshops
P.O. Box 1028
Concord, MA 01742

Shaker-style rockers and chairs in kits or already assembled.

Wave Hill Lawn Furniture
675 West 252nd Street
Bronx, NY 10471

Unfinished pine lawn chair based on modernistic Gerrit Rietveld design.

Willow Works
209 Glen Cove Avenue
Sea Cliff, NY 11579

Bent-willow chairs, lounges, swings, and plant stands, stripped, dyed, or plain.

Willsboro Wood Products
P.O. Box 336
Willsboro, NY 12996

Rustic cedar rockers, lounges, settees, tables, and Adirondack chairs.

Wood Classics
RD #1, Box 455E
High Falls, NY 12440

Mahogany and teak benches, chairs, picnic tables, and lounges; swings, poolside rockers, and Adirondack furniture.

Zona
97 Greene Street
New York, NY 10012

English teak furniture and a selection of furniture and accessories from the American Southwest.

Greenhouses, Gazebos, Small Buildings

Columbine
P.O. Box 212
Route 3
Blairstown, NJ 07825

Modular terracotta columns in a variety of colors which can be put together to make pergolas and gazebos.

The English Garden
Machin Designs USA, Inc.
652 Glenbrook Road
Stamford, CT 06906

Freestanding and attached conservatories inspired by Victorian designs.

Four Seasons Greenhouses
425 Smith Street
Farmingdale, NY 11735

Aluminum-framed sunrooms and greenhouses with single-, double-, or triple-glazing.

Janco Greenhouses
J.A. Nearing Co.
9390 Davis Avenue
Laurel, MD 20707

Greenhouses and sunrooms with aluminum framing.

Lord & Burnham
2 Main Street
Irvington, NY 10533

Extensive range of aluminum-framed sunrooms and greenhouses.

Walpole Woodworkers
767 East Street
Walpole, MA 02081

Several small wooden garden sheds and buildings in kit form; also cabanas, boathouses, and stables.

Zytco Solariums
825 Denison Street, Unit 16
Markham, Ontario L3R 5E4
Canada

*Custom-made aluminum-framed solariums and sunrooms
with double-, triple-, or heat-treated glazing.*

LIGHTING

Genie House
P.O. Box 2478
Red Lion Road
Vincetown, NJ 08088

Hand-crafted garden lamps in solid brass and copper.

Hammerworks
6 Fremont Street
Worcester, MA 01603

*Post and wall-mounted electric lanterns, handmade and
finished in copper or brass.*

Philip Hawk & Company
159 East College Avenue
Pleasant Gap, PA 16823

Stone lanterns hand-carved in granite.

Heritage Lanterns
70A Main Street
Yarmouth, ME 04096

*Pewter, copper, and brass lanterns in Colonial styles; post
and wall-mounted models.*

Idaho Wood
P.O. Box 488
Sandpoint, ID 83864

Cedar landscape and wall lights.

Popovitch and Associates, Inc.
346 Ashland Avenue
Pittsburgh, PA 15228

*Unusual outdoor lamps with copper stems and ceramic
globes—bell-shaped, mushroom-shaped, bud-shaped.*

Rab Electrical Manufacturing Company, Inc.
321 Ryder Avenue
Bronx, NY 10451

Security and general outdoor lighting.

Wendelighting
2445 North Naomi Street
Burbank, CA 91504

*Plant lights, tree illumination, and other kinds of
landscape lighting.*

NURSERIES AND SEED CATALOGS

The Antique Rose Emporium
Box 143
Route 5
Brenham, TX 77833

Good selection of old-fashioned roses.

Beaverlodge Nurseries
Box 127
Beaverlodge, Alberta T0H 0C0
Canada

*Large selection of hardy ornamental and fruit trees,
shrubs, and perennials suitable for northern regions.*

Kurt Bluemel, Inc.
2740 Greene Lane
Baldwin, MD 21013

*Over one hundred varieties of ornamental grasses and
rushes, as well as bamboos, ferns, and perennials.*

Burpee Seed Co.
Warminster, PA 18991

*One of the oldest and largest mail-order suppliers; wide
range of vegetable and flower seeds, as well as shrubs
and fruit trees.*

Carlson's Gardens
P.O. Box 305
South Salem, NY 10590

Selection of azaleas, mountain laurels, and rhododendrons.

Herb Gathering, Inc.
5742 Kenwood Avenue
Kansas City, MO 64110

Herb plants and seeds and hard-to-find vegetables.

Jackson and Perkins Co.
83A Rose Lane
Medford, OR 97501

Roses and fruit trees.

Klehm Nursery
P.O. Box 197
Route 5
South Barrington, IL 60010

*Extensive selection of bearded iris, day lilies, hostas,
and peonies.*

Lilypons Water Gardens
P.O. Box 10
Lilypons, MD 21717

*Water lilies, water grasses, and bog plants, ornamental
fish, ponds, and pond supplies.*

Logee's Greenhouses
55 North Street
Danielson, CT 06239

*Geraniums and begonias; herbs, mosses, and ferns;
perennials.*

Nor'East Miniature Roses, Inc.
58 Hammond Street
Rowley, MA 01969

Wide selection of miniature roses.

Pickering Nurseries
670 Kingston Road
Pickering, Ontario L1V 1A6
Canada

Good selection of old-fashioned roses.

Richters
Box 26
Goodwood, Ontario L0C 1A0
Canada

*Exceptional source for herb seeds and plants including
many unusual and hard-to-find varieties.*

Roses of Yesterday and Today
802 Brown's Valley Road
Watsonville, CA 95076

Extensive range of old-fashioned roses.

John Scheepers, Inc.
63 Wall Street
New York, NY 10005

Seasonal selections of daffodils, tulips, and other bulbs.

Swan Island Dahlias
P.O. Box 800
Candy, OR 97013

Good assortment of dwarf and giant dahlias.

Van Bourgondian Bros.
P.O. Box A
245 Route 109
Babylon, NY 11702

Good selection of Dutch bulbs.

Van Ness Water Gardens
2460 North Euclid Avenue
Upland, CA 91768

Water lilies, fountains, filters, and pond supplies.

Vermont Wildflower Farm
P.O. Box 5
Charlotte, VT 05445

Various wildflower species, plus wildflower mixes.

Wayside Gardens
Hodges, SC 29695

*All-around selection of plants, bulbs, shrubs, and trees;
some garden tools and furniture.*

Woodland Nurseries
2152 Camilla Road
Mississauga, Ontario L5A 2K1
Canada

*Alpine perennials, evergreens, and especially ornamental
trees and shrubs: dogwoods, azaleas, rhododendrons,
and magnolias.*

ACKNOWLEDGMENTS

Numerous people contributed their time and thoughts toward the book. Many went out of their way to show us backyards, and others shared ideas and advice; in particular we would like to thank J. Hyde Crawford. We wish to express our gratitude to the homeowners and to these professionals whose yards appear in this book for their generous hospitality and enthusiastic support. Without their help this book could not have existed.

Bates, Booher, Lund
Architects
Watermill, New York 11976

Jack Ceglic
Designer
New York, New York 10012

Mark Enos
Designer
Los Angeles, California 90069

Frederick Fisher
Architect
Santa Monica, California 90401

Mariette Himes Gomez
Interior Designer
New York, New York 10021

Raymond Gomez
Architect
New York, New York 10021

Caroline Guttilla
Interior Designer
Locust Valley, New York 11560

Mary MacDonald
Landscape Gardener
Locust Valley, New York 11560

Christine Maly
Interior Designer
New York, New York 10022

Randolph Marshall
Landscape Architect
Katonah, New York 10536

Moore Ruble Yudell
Architects and Planners
Santa Monica, California 90404

Brian A. Murphy
Architect
Pacific Palisades, California 90272

Luis Ortega
Designer
Los Angeles, California 90048

Ivy Reid
Landscape Designer
Pacific Palisades, California 90272

Rios Pearson, Inc.
Architects and Landscape Architects
Los Angeles, California 90036

Joseph Ruggiero
Designer
Fairfield, Connecticut 06430

Richard L. Segal
Landscape Designer
Hollywood, California 90028

Lisa Stamm
Landscape Gardener
Shelter Island, New York 11965

Dan Stewart
Landscape Architect
New York, New York 10011

Smallwood and Stewart would like to thank Katherine Barrett for her tireless research and attention to detail, Mike Rose for creating such an effective and beautiful design, Sue Rose for her invaluable last-minute help, and Nancy Kenmore for two frantic days of inspired catering.

Many people have contributed to the book at Viking Penguin, and in particular we would like to thank: Alicia Sinclair, Victoria Meyer, Brenda Marsh, and Christine Ramos; and most important, Barbara Williams, for keeping such firm and steady control even when time was short, and Michael Fragnito, for understanding and giving unfailing support to the book from the very start.